The BIG Book of AFRICAN AMERICAN Activities

SCHOOL OF EDUCATION
CURRICULUM LABORATORY
UM-DEARBORN

by Carole Marsh

Editorial Assistant: Jenny Corsey • Graphic Design: Cecil Anderson & Lynette Rowe

Published by

GALLOPADE™
INTERNATIONAL

800-536-2GET
www.gallopade.com

Gallopade is proud to be a member of these educational organizations and associations:

**The National School Supply and Equipment Association
The National Council for the Social Studies
Association for Supervision and Curriculum Development
Museum Store Association
Association of Partners for Public Lands**

Black Jazz, Pizzazz, & Razzmatazz Books

Our Black Heritage Coloring Book

Black Heritage GameBook: Keep Score! Have Fun!
Find out how much you already know—and learn lots more!

Black Trivia: The African American Experience A-to-Z!

Celebrating Black Heritage:
20 Days of Activities, Reading, Recipes, Parties, Plays, and More!

Mini Timeline of Awesome African American Achievements and Events

"Let's Quilt Our African American Heritage & Stuff It Topographically!"

The Best Book of Black Biographies

The Color Purple & All That Jazz!: African American Achievements in the Arts

"Out of the Mouths of Slaves": African American Oral History

The Kitchen House: How Yesterday's Black Women Created Today's
Most Popular & Famous American Foods!

Black Business: African American Entrepreneurs & Their Amazing Success!

Other Carole Marsh Books

Meet Shirley Franklin: Mayor of Atlanta!

Kwanzaa Activities, Crafts, Recipes, and More!

African American Readers—Many to choose from!

A Word From the Author

Dear Kids,

African American heritage is a very special history. Almost everything about African Americans is interesting and fun! This group of people shares a remarkable past that helped create the great nation of America. African Americans are unique and have accomplished many important things for our country.

This Activity Book is chock-full of activities to motivate you to learn more about African Americans. While completing puzzles, coloring activities, searching through word finds, and other fun activities, you will learn more about African American heritage, geography, history, people, places, and more.

Whether you're sitting in a classroom, riding in the backseat of a car, or doing pages for fun in your room, I hope that you have as much fun using this Activity Book as I did writing it!

Enjoy learning about African American heritage – it's the educational journey of a lifetime!

Carole Marsh

National Historic Landmarks

Use the picture clues to match each famous African American historic landmark with its name. Use the clues to help you!

African Meeting House
(known as Abolition Church)
Boston, Massachusetts
(photo 1937) _____

First Church of Christ
(Slaves from the ship
Amistad were educated
here during their trial)
Farmington, Connecticut
(photo 1976) _____

Robert Brown Elliot School
(Colored School No. 9)
Baltimore, Maryland
(photo 1985) _____

Culpepper Courthouse
Culpepper, Virginia
(photo 1862) _____

Martin Luther King, Jr.
(birth home)
Atlanta, Georgia
(photo 1980) _____

Black History Month!

Carter G. Woodson, an American historian, sought a way to emphasize the importance of Negro history. He created Negro History Week (later to become Black History Month). Now America celebrates Black History Month every February. During this month, we recognize the great accomplishments and important events of African Americans. We are grateful for their contributions, sacrifices, and service to our country. America looks forward to future generations of citizens working together in peace.

Fill in each day of Black History Month with an important African American achievement or event. Some have been done already to help get you started. Celebrate each day of Black History Month by remembering these and other important contributions of African Americans!

FEBRUARY

1	2	3	4	5	6	7
Hank Aaron was given the Spingarn Award for baseball achievements.	Hiram Revels became the first black U.S. Senator in 1870.	Blacks first met to form the NAACP in 1909.	Thomas Peterson was the first Black to vote under the 15th Amendment.	Black statesman Frederick Douglass was born in 1817.		
8	9	10	11	12	13	14
15	16	17	18	19	20	21
22	23	24	25	26	27	28

Getting To Know The Land Called Africa!

Africa is the second largest continent. It is a land filled with wildlife, grasslands, rain forests, and natural riches such as gold and diamonds. Africa contains the world's largest desert (the Sahara) and the world's longest river (the Nile)!

1. Connect the dots with a green crayon.

2. Color the Sahara Desert red.

3. Color the Nile River blue.

4. Color the rest of Africa yellow.

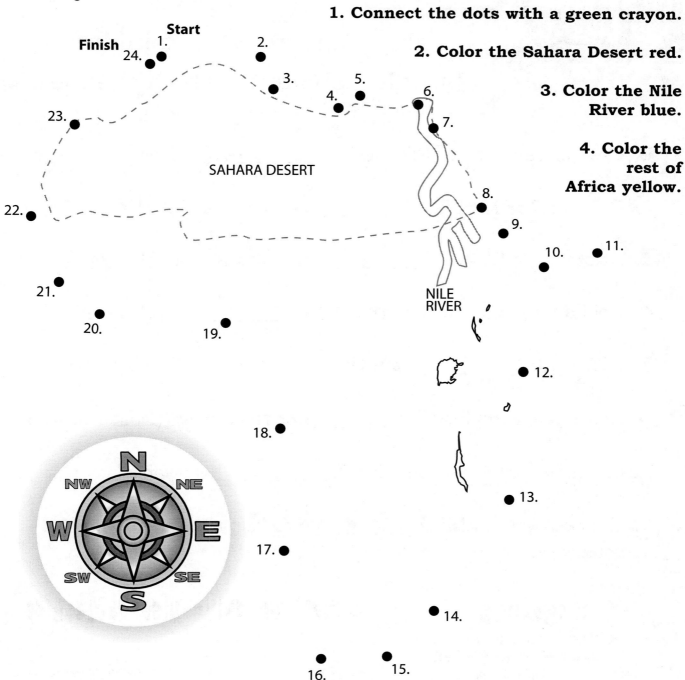

SAHARA DESERT

NILE RIVER

Start
Finish

African Proverbs

Unscramble the words below! Where each proverb originated from is written in parentheses.

WORD BANK

ship   friend   bed   children
bundle   shelters   strong   hands

1. To be united is to be NGSROT _____. (Africa)

2. The roof RSSTEHEL _____ the whole family. (Hausa)

3. Sticks in a UNDBLE _____ are unbreakable. (Kenya)

4. Hold a true friend with both ASNHD _____. (Nigeria)

5. CDREILNH _____ are the wisdom of the nation. (Liberia)

6. Home is a warm EBD _____ for the family. (South Africa)

7. One man cannot launch a HISP _____. (Swahili)

8. You need your FENRID _____ to help put the firewood on your back. (Zulu)

Quote

"For if one lost, all lost—the chain that held them would save all or none."
— Toni Morrison

Answer Key: 1-strong, 2-shelters, 3-bundle, 4-hands, 5-children, 6-bed, 7-ship, 8-friend

Who Discovered the North Pole?!

North Pole

In the early 1900s, many people wanted to be the first to discover the North Pole. Explorer Robert Peary led an Arctic expedition in 1909 to find the Pole. Robert asked Matthew Henson, a black explorer, to be his partner. The American explorers battled harsh winds and cold temperatures (as low as 60 degrees below zero!) with the help of dogs and Eskimos. The group split up to search in different directions.

Matthew Henson discovered the North Pole first! Robert asked Matthew not to speak publicly about his discovery because Matthew was black. Robert was given credit for Matthew's discovery. The President even made Robert an admiral. Everyone received medals except for Matthew, even the cook! After the discovery, Matthew worked in a parking garage until some black politicians found him a better job as a messenger. His accomplishments were not recognized until many years later.

Use information from the paragraph above to complete the crossword.

1. Robert Peary was an American _____. (DOWN)

2. Lt. Peary asked Matthew to join his Arctic _____. (ACROSS)

3. Matthew Henson discovered the _____ Pole first! (ACROSS)

4. Lt. Peary asked Matthew _____ not to speak publicly about his discovery. (DOWN)

5. Everyone received a _____ except for Matthew, who was black. (ACROSS)

Answers: (1) explorer; (2) expedition; (3) North; (4) Henson; (5) medal

Inspiring Puppets!

Cut out the faces of these inspirational black leaders of yesterday and today. Glue them onto craft sticks. Write speeches for each puppet.

Thurgood Marshall

Frederick Douglass

Colin Powell

Sojourner Truth

Martin Luther King, Jr.

Booker T. Washington

Rosa Parks

Have a puppet parade!

One Small Step... One Giant Leap!

African American astronauts are taking leaps and bounds in the NASA
program. Their contributions launched new steps into space for America.

ASTRONAUT	SPACECRAFT	WOW!	DATE
1. Mae Jemison	Endeavor	first black woman in space!	1992
2. Frederick Gregory	Discovery	first black Space Commander!	1989
3. Charles Bolden	Discovery	helped launch Hubble space telescope!	1990
4. Guion Bluford	Challenger	first African American in space!	1983
5. Bernard Harris	Discovery	first African American to walk in space!	1995
6. Ronald McNair	Challenger	killed in Challenger launch explosion	1986
7. Michael Anderson	Endeavor	active astronaut today!	1998
8. Winston Scott	Endeavor	performed gravity experiment in space!	1996

**Put the above years into chronological order. Then write them in that order
on the planets (1-8) around the universe. Use the blanks.**

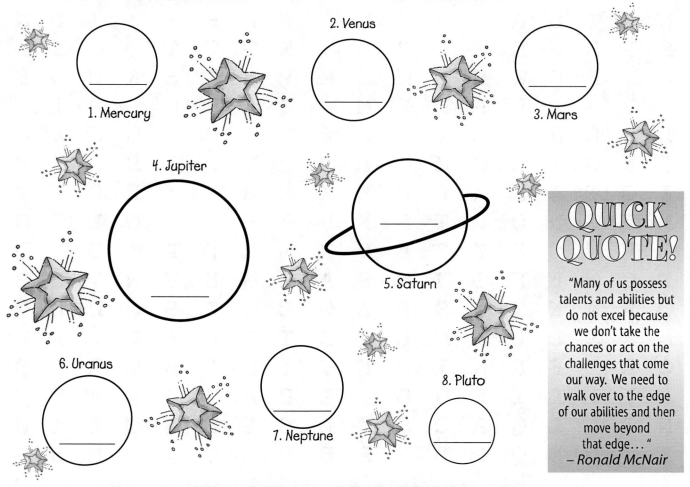

1. Mercury
2. Venus
3. Mars
4. Jupiter
5. Saturn
6. Uranus
7. Neptune
8. Pluto

QUICK QUOTE!

"Many of us possess
talents and abilities but
do not excel because
we don't take the
chances or act on the
challenges that come
our way. We need to
walk over to the edge
of our abilities and then
move beyond
that edge... "
– Ronald McNair

Jazzy, Pizzazzy, Razzamatazzy Word Search

African Americans have contributed to the jazz scene in American music more than any other ethnic group. The words below include legendary singers and musicians, and famous jazz hotspots.

WORD BANK

Find the words.

Ella Fitzgerald
Louis Armstrong
Fats Waller
Cotton Club
New Orleans

Duke Ellington
Fletcher Henderson
Jelly Roll Morton
Harlem
Memphis

Billie Holiday
Dizzy Gillespie
Greenwich Village
Queens
South Chicago

```
F L E T C H E R H E N D E R S O N D
D A Q P G R O G A C I H C H T U O S
U K T U R T D F R E J B F T Z I D N
K N S S E H B U L C N O T T O C E K
E I B O W E E M E M P H I S K W D E
E T A P E A N F M I Z A R C O P I A
L F E J G R L S C P Z T H R S J Z J
L N O T R O M L L O R Y L L E J Z F
I O T E S X P K E K H E E I E O Y T
N V G N O R T S M R A S I U O L G G
G V W O Y Z Z A V N N R F P A U I H
T C W E F I J N S A I N H E N T L B
O R A N T W S P E G E C T S Q U L P
N F S D L A R E G Z T I F A L L E F
G R E E N W I C H V I L L A G E S Q
B I L L I E H O L I D A Y P A F P C
N I L L Q A O S C L S Y E Y U L I U
X Z L B Q S L Y A E M M O I P M E S
```

First Living Trademark

Nancy Green was born in Montgomery County, Kentucky. She was a poor slave. Nancy loved to make pancakes and wanted others to try them. In 1893, when the Columbian Exposition came to Chicago, she decided to serve pancakes in a booth to see what people thought of them. The people loved Nancy's pancakes! She invented the first pancake flour mix for commercial use. At age 59, Nancy became "Aunt Jemima," the world's first living trademark!

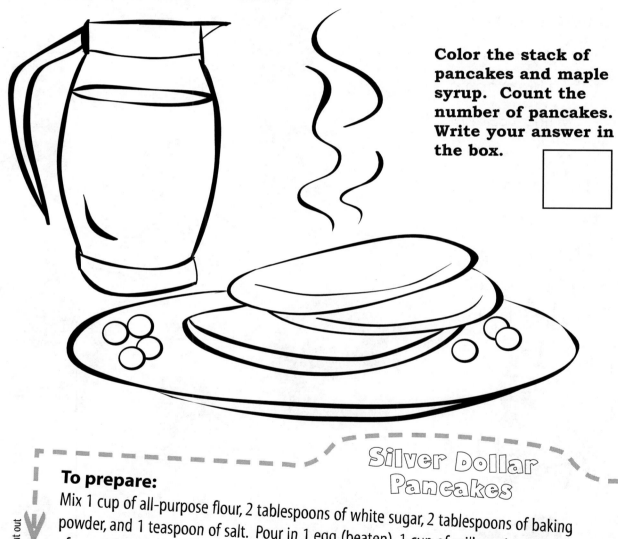

Color the stack of pancakes and maple syrup. Count the number of pancakes. Write your answer in the box.

Silver Dollar Pancakes

Cut out

To prepare:
Mix 1 cup of all-purpose flour, 2 tablespoons of white sugar, 2 tablespoons of baking powder, and 1 teaspoon of salt. Pour in 1 egg (beaten), 1 cup of milk, and 2 tablespoons of vegetable oil. Mix until smooth. Heat a griddle over medium high heat or 375°F. Pour small circles of batter onto the griddle. Brown on both sides and serve warm with maple syrup, butter, or freshly whipped cream and fruit topping.

Hard at Work

Match these hardworking African Americans with their jobs.

Put an A by the computer operator.

Put a B by the nurse.

Put a C by the carpenter.

Put a D by the architect.

Put an E by the graphic designer

Put an F by the teacher.

Put an G by the athlete.

Put an H by the soldier.

Put a I by the chef.

Put an J by the singer.

Put a K by the musician.

Put a L by the jet pilot.

Let It Wave!

Marcus Garvey, a famous African American leader, created a new flag for black people in the early 1900s. This new flag was called a bendera. A red stripe at the top symbolizes the difficult struggle for freedom and equality. A black stripe in the middle represents unity and encourages the black community to stay together. The green stripe stands for the future!

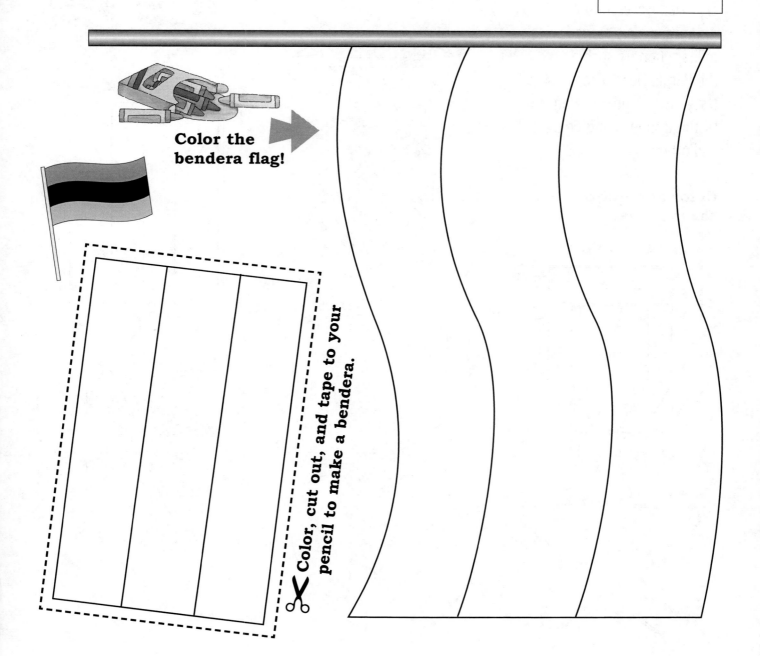

Color the bendera flag!

Color, cut out, and tape to your pencil to make a bendera.

Medals of Honor

African Americans have served our country bravely in many wars, including the American Revolution and the Civil War. Several African Americans have earned military honors, such as the Purple Heart, Bronze Star, Navy Cross, Medal of Honor, Distinguished Flying Cross, and others.

Color and cut out these medals.

VALOR

UNITED · STATES · OF · AMERICA

Continuing an Oral Tradition!

Most slaves could not read or write. They passed down their history by singing spirituals and telling stories. Many cultures have practiced this oral form of communication, and some still do today!

Ask an older African American for an interview. Perhaps you could talk with a grandparent, a friend, or a teacher! Ask this person some of the questions below. Ask some of your own questions too! Think about your interview. What new things did you learn?

1. Where and when were you born? Describe your hometown.
2. What were your parents like? What did they teach you?
3. Please describe some experiences from your school days.
4. What were some of your favorite things to do when you were growing up?
5. Did you ever experience discrimination because of your race?

6. _____

7. _____

Write a short paragraph (at least 3-4 sentences!) that tells the story of the person that you interviewed.

_____

_____

_____

_____

_____

_____

_____

Listening + Doing + Thinking = Learning

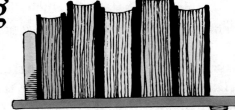

Complete the math problems to discover what year these amazing academic achievements occurred.

1. Richard Theodore Greener is the first African American to graduate from Harvard University.

$600 + 475 + 125 - 45 + 395 + 455 + 25 - 160 = $ _____

2. African American Booker T. Washington leads Tuskegee Institute.

$550 + 325 + 650 - 90 + 225 + 900 - 400 - 279 = $ _____

3. African American Fanny Jackson Coppins starts a school for African American students.

$100 + 875 + 505 - 120 + 425 + 600 - 425 - 72 = $ _____

4. African American Mary McLeod Bethune founds an African American college.

$125 + 240 + 775 - 30 + 635 + 720 - 400 - 161 = $ _____

5. Alain Leroy Locke is the first African American Rhodes Scholar.

$195 + 780 + 435 - 60 + 75 + 845 - 300 - 63 = $ _____

6. Eva Beatrice Dykes is the first African American woman to finish her Ph.D. requirements.

$55 + 895 + 200 - 20 + 715 + 125 + 25 - 74 = $ _____

7. Six-year-old Ruby Bridges is the first black child to desegregate a white school.

$90 + 45 + 880 - 75 + 495 + 525 + 80 - 80 = $ _____

Answers: 1-1870; 2-1881; 3-1888; 4-1904; 5-1907; 6-1921; 7-1960

Set Us Free!

The Emancipation Proclamation of 1863 set the African American slaves free! Which popular president issued this proclamation?

Draw a circle around the correct president. Color the presidents.

Abraham Lincoln

John F. Kennedy

Franklin D. Roosevelt

Jimmy Carter

George Washington

Thomas Jefferson

Answer: Abraham Lincoln

Business Code Buster

Solve the codes to find out the names of some successful African American businesspeople.

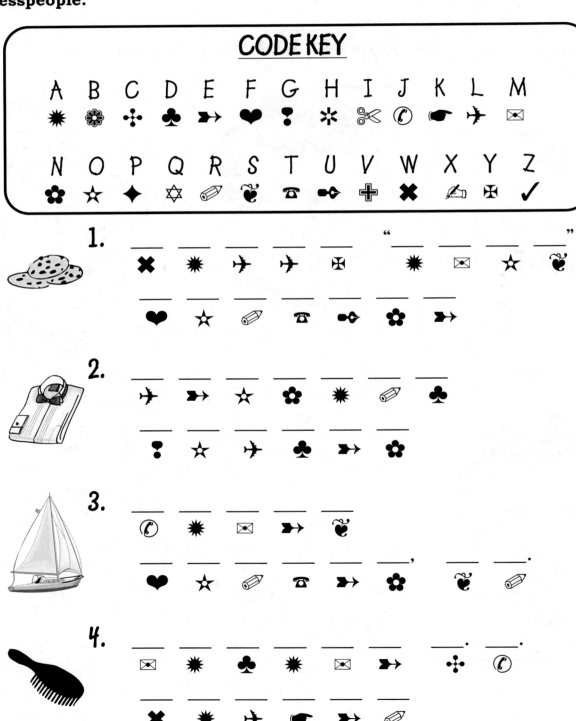

At Last, At Last... Free at Last!

The Emancipation Proclamation

President Abraham Lincoln delivered the Emancipation Proclamation on January 1, 1863 during the Civil War. He said that all slaves in America were free! That also meant that owning slaves was illegal. This was one of the many reasons why the Northern and Southern states fought each other. After being set free, more than 200,000 black men joined the Union army to fight. Almost 40,000 black soldiers died serving their country in the Civil War.

Use the Word Bank to fill in the sentence blanks.

WORD BANK

1863	Civil	freed
Union	40,000	Lincoln

The "Juneteenth Celebration" remembers the ending of slavery.

1. The Emancipation Proclamation _____ the black slaves!

2. After gaining freedom, black men could fight in the _____ army.

3. Nearly _____ black soldiers died in the Civil War.

4. The _____ War was fought between the North and South.

5. President Abraham _____ delivered the Emancipation Proclamation in January of _____.

FAST FACT
Blacks suffered discrimination even in the Union Army! Black soldiers received $7 monthly pay, but white soldiers were paid $13 a month. Blacks strongly protested against the unfair pay rate. Congress changed the law in 1864 to require that black and white soldiers receive equal pay.

African American Spelling Bee!

Good spelling is a good habit!

Study the words on the page. Most all of them can be found within the activities in this book! Then fold the right half of the page under. Take a "spelling test!" Ask a friend to read the words aloud to you. Write the correct spelling on the line. When finished, unfold the page and check your spelling. How many did you spell right? Study the words you miss.

WORDS:

freedom
ignorance
leader
Africa
escape
jazz
King
discrimination
poet
ship
Tuskegee
black
emancipation
slave
proclamation
racism
boycott
Olympian
civil rights

A B C D E

Streeeeeeeetch!

"Pull apart" these sentences to find out some cool trivia about African Americans! Write your answer on the lines provided.

1. WilliamAlexanderLeidesdorffwasthefirstAfricanAmericanmillionaireand thefirstknownblackdiplomatintheUnitedStates.

_____

_____

_____

2. DorieMillerwasawardedtheNavyCrossforhisheroismduringthePearl Harborattack.

_____

_____

_____

3. WriterRalphEllisonwonthe1952NationalBookAwardforhisInvisibleMan novel.

_____

_____

_____

4. LieutenantGeneralBenjaminO.DavisJr.,aWestPointgraduate,becamethe firstblackAirForcegeneralin1954.

_____

_____

_____

Quilting Bee!

Black slave women created quilts to tell their life stories for decades. Their quilts encouraged friendship, provided comfort and beauty, and expressed joy or sadness. Some special quilts even gave secret directions on the "Underground Railroad" to runaway slaves. The art of quilt making has survived time, technology, and changing fashion.

Think about the most important events of your life. Perhaps your first day of school or when you won a special award! Maybe the day your family welcomed a new brother or sister. Don't forget your first birthday! Draw colorful picture that represents each event - in order - inside the nine quilt squares. Use the last square to illustrate the future! You will create a beautiful story quilt of your life!

Symbol Scramble

Write the correct number next to each African American symbol.

___ Tuskegee Airmen patch   ___ Black History Month   ___ kente cloth

___ jazz musician's trumpet   ___ Spingarn Medal   ___ Poet Maya Angelou's pen

Embrace African Heritage!

Africa hosts one of the world's most diverse collection of people and cultures. The land is rich in natural resources, wildlife, and ethnic heritage. Africa is the second largest continent in the world and the only one to exist in all hemispheres. Aside from the mountains (Kilimanjaro) and deserts (Sahara), the terrain is a grassy home to a greater range of animals than any other part of the world.

America benefits from the diverse, or different, ethnic origins that make up the American people. We can learn about each other's heritage. In this way, we share our diversity. Name one example for each category below that represents African heritage!

1. Holiday: _____

2. Food: _____

3. Clothing: _____

4. Religion: _____

5. Music: _____

6. Economy: _____

7. Wildlife: _____

8. Military: _____

9. Attraction: _____

---

diverse: different or varied

ethnic: a group of people who have the same language, culture, or religion

custom: a way of doing something that has been accepted among a group of people

Places To Go! Things To Do!

African Americans have left their mark all over our great nation. There are lots of fun places to visit in America where you can learn more about black heritage and accomplishments.

Match the cities with their states by drawing a line to connect them!

- The Civil Rights Institute, Birmingham
- Museum of the National Center of Afro-American Artists, Boston
- Amistad Research Center, New Orleans
- Tuskegee Airmen National Museum, Detroit
- Martin Luther King, Jr. National Historic Site, Atlanta
- Black American West Museum & Heritage Center, Denver
- National Civil Rights Museum, Memphis
- Greensboro Historical Museum, Greensboro
- African American Museum of Fine Arts, San Diego

Tennessee

Massachusetts

Georgia

Louisiana

Alabama

California

Colorado

North Carolina

Michigan

African Americans in Government Hunt!

Many African Americans serve as public servants in the U.S. government. Their jobs are very important because they help make sure our country stays safe and free!

Below is a list of some African Americans who have served or are serving in U.S. government. Go on a scavenger hunt and research one fact about each person such as a job title, award, or special accomplishment. Use an encyclopedia, almanac, library book, the Internet, or even an expert!

General Colin Powell   <u>U.S Secretary of State</u>

Hon. Clarence Thomas _____

Senator J.C. Watts _____

Condoleezza Rice _____

Dr. Ralph Bunche _____

Jefferson Long _____

Harold Ford, Jr. _____

David Dinkins _____

John M. Langston _____

Charles Hayes _____

Rod Paige _____

John Lewis _____

Robert Smalls _____

Bobby Rush _____

Thurgood Marshall _____

Harold Washington _____

Wellington Webb _____

L. Douglas Wilder _____

Shirley Chisholm _____

Proud to Be an African American!

African Americans originate from many different countries. They first came to America as slaves.

Blacks helped win their freedom by fighting in the Civil War. They worked hard to help others realize their new rights.

Today African Americans are an integral part of U.S. culture through literature, sports, government, academia, fine arts, science, and more.

The basic principles of our government serve to unite Americans, who are all entitled to enjoy the rights to life, liberty, and the pursuit of happiness; and equality under the law.

WORD WHEEL

liberty · law · equality · unite · traditions · life · African · different · happiness · nations

Read the paragraph. Use the Word Wheel to fill in the blanks.

_____ Americans come from many different _____. They bring their own _____ customs and _____. Individual rights to _____, _____, and the pursuit of _____; and _____ under the _____ are the basic principles that form the United States government. These are the principles that _____ all Americans.

ANSWERS: African, nations, different, traditions, life, liberty, happiness, equality, law, unite

Riding, Roping, and Rodeos!

About 9,000 black cowboys helped drive big herds of cattle West after the Civil War. Black and white cowboys worked, ate, and slept together. Though racial discrimination still existed, black workers were treated much better on the range than most anywhere else. Skills mattered to the rancher bosses, and the black cowboys proved themselves valuable on the ranch. Then black cowboys used those skills in the popular local rodeos to participate in exciting events like riding bulls and bucking broncos!

Label the rodeo gear. Use the Word Bank.

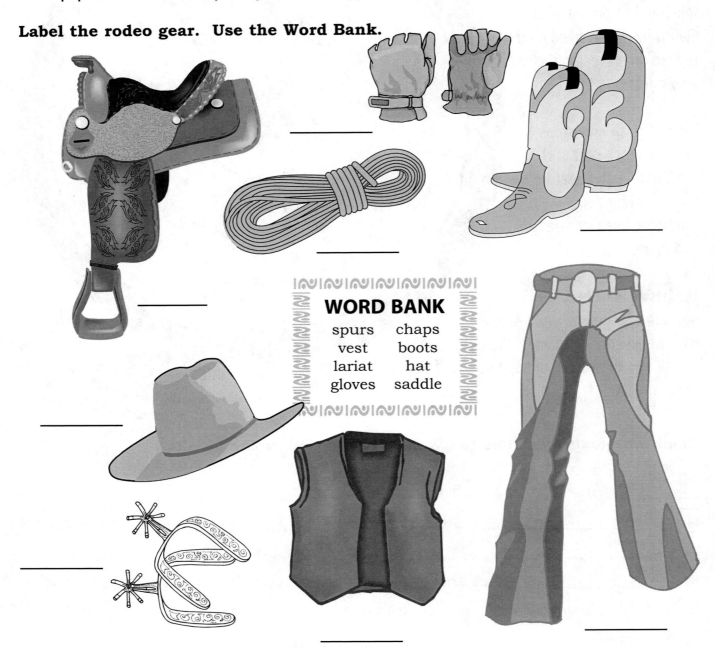

WORD BANK

spurs	chaps
vest	boots
lariat	hat
gloves	saddle

What a Great Idea!

Inventors watch how things work in the world. They think about how to make things better. Their ideas help make the world safer, easier, or more efficient. Many black inventors have improved people's lives with their creative inventions. Complete the activity below to find out more about a few of the most famous black inventors.

Match each inventor with the correct invention. Use the picture clues!

INVENTOR

____ Garrett Morgan

____ Henry Blair

____ Jan Matzeliger

____ Lewis Latimer

____ Elijah McCoy

____ Joseph Winters

____ Granville Woods

____ Jerry Certain

____ Benjamin Banneker

____ George Grant

____ Phillip Downing

____ John Albert Burr

INVENTION

A. Lubrication for Steam Engine

B. Traffic Light

C. Electric Light Bulb Filament

D. Wooden Clock

E. Shoe Sole Sewing Machine

F. Bicycle Basket

G. Golf Tee

H. Big Blue Mailbox (public use)

I. Railway Telegraph

J. Fire Escape Ladder

K. Corn Planter

L. Lawnmower (device to keep grass from clogging gears)

Answers: B, K, E, C, A, J, I, F, D, G, H, L

Soul Food

Hundreds of years ago, black slave women did most of the cooking for white families, especially in the South. They creatively used spices from nature and invented new recipes. Many of these recipes are now known as "soul food." Everyone can enjoy them today!

WORD BANK

sweet potato pone	okra	succotash	sassafras
collards	black-eyed peas	hominy	fried chicken
cornbread	cabbage	red-eye gravy	grits
benne seeds	pecan pie	peaches	boiled peanuts
chitlins	molasses	yam pudding	gumbo

Use the Word Bank of recipes and ingredients to complete the crossword puzzle.

From One Continent to Another!

The ancestors of African Americans were brought from Africa to the United States on slave ships. Conditions were very unhealthy and cruel aboard the ships. Many slaves died during the long trip. Sometimes Europeans captured Africans as slaves, but Africans also sold their own people as slaves. Families were divided, and African tribes were changed forever.

Use a red crayon to trace a path through the maze. Color Africa green. Then color the United States blue. The United States is part of the North American continent. Don't forget Alaska and Hawaii too! Color the other countries in North America yellow.

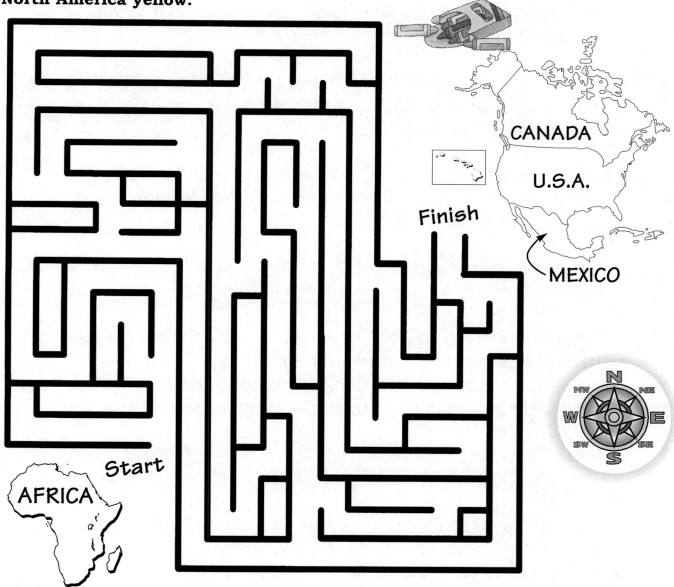

Amazing Olympic Athletes!

Have you ever dreamed of winning a medal in the international Olympic Games? African American athletes have brought several Olympic medals home to America over the years! Some black athletes have also made America proud by breaking *world records* at the Olympic events!

Number the Olympic medallists in the correct order, ending with the most recent year.

_____ Carl Lewis is one of only 4 Olympic athletes to win 9 gold medals. He competed in several track and field events in 4 separate Olympic Games. Carl's last Olympic competition was in **1996**.

_____ Florence Griffith-Joyner won 3 gold medals at the **1988** Olympic Games. She also won 2 silver medals in the previous Olympics. Florence's fans nicknamed her Flojo and would cheer "Go Flo!"

_____ Marion Jones won 5 medals in track and field events in the **2000** Olympic Games. She became the first woman to ever win 5 medals in the same Olympics!

_____ Bob Beamon won a gold medal at the **1968** Olympic Games. He broke the long jump world record by leaping 29 feet & 2 1/2 inches!

_____ Wilma Rudolph won 3 gold medals in track and field events in the **1960** Olympics. She also won a bronze medal in her first Olympic competition — at age 16! Wilma overcame polio, scarlet fever, and pneumonia to become an American Olympic heroine!

_____ Jesse Owens broke 5 world records in track and field events during the **1936** Olympic Games. He won 4 gold medals!

_____ In **2002**, Vonetta Flowers became the first African American to win an Olympic gold medal in the Winter Games. She was part of a two-woman bobsleigh team.

Answers: 5, 4, 6, 3, 2, 1, 7

Carver's Treats!

George Washington Carver is remembered as one of America's greatest scientists. This African American farming wizard figured out how to create more than 300 products from peanuts, and many products from sweet potatoes and pecans! Carver also directed the agricultural department at Tuskegee Industrial Institute in Alabama. He told farmers to plant different crops each year to help put nutrients back into the soil. Carver's discoveries and ideas made the farming industry grow and grow and grow in the South!

Match the name of each food George Washington Carver improved with its picture.

sweet potato

pecans

peanuts

1. Carver created ice cream and sugar from:
   a. wheat and barley
   b. peanut butter and jelly
   c. sweet potatoes and peanuts

2. Carver was also known as:
   a. an excellent speaker
   b. a famous politician
   c. a classical musician

3. Congress honored Carver with:
   a. the first federal monument dedicated to a black person
   b. a government position
   c. a science award

4. Carver became the first black graduate of:
   a. Howard University
   b. Harvard University
   c. Iowa State University

FAST FACT

More Stuff George Washington Carver Created From Plants... bleach, marble, shaving cream, dye, cheese, shampoo, instant coffee, shoe polish, mayonnaise, buttermilk, ink, chili sauce, paper, sugar, rubber, even steak sauce! But believe it or not... George did not discover peanut butter!

Answers: 1-c; 2-a; 3-a; 4-c

Word Factory

**Let's brainstorm! Write as many words as you
can from the letters in the phrase below.**

"BLACK HISTORY!"

_____   _____

_____   _____

_____   _____

_____   _____

_____   _____

_____   _____

_____   _____

_____   _____

_____   _____

_____   _____

_____   _____

Black Cabinet Leaders!

The President of the United States appoints a "cabinet" after winning an election. Members of the presidential cabinet are asked to support and advise the president. Other people are also asked to help in specific positions. President George W. Bush asked many important black leaders to provide their individual experience and knowledge so that he can do his job better. The President and all his helpers make sure that we can live in peace and safety in our great country!

Rod Paige

Colin Powell

Condoleezza Rice

Unscramble the words to discover facts about each U.S. leader.

FACTS ABOUT OUR BLACK LEADERS

1. Colin Powell was appointed the first black U.S. Secretary of TTSAE _____.

2. Rod Paige was appointed U.S. Secretary of DTEUCAION _____.

3. Colin Powell served in Persian FGLU _____ War as a Four-star General.

4. Condoleezza Rice was appointed National Security Advisor to the ESRPINTEDE _____.

5. Rod Paige once worked as head BLLAFTOO _____ coach at Jackson State University.

6. Condoleezza Rice trained as a competitive ice KTERSA _____ and concert pianist.

Answers: 1. State, 2. Education, 3. Gulf, 4. President, 5. football, 6. skater

Where In The World Is Africa?

Africa is a continent made up of many countries. North America only has three countries! A hemisphere is one half of the earth. The Equator divides the earth into the Northern Hemisphere and the Southern Hemisphere. The Prime Meridian divides the earth into the Eastern Hemisphere and the Western Hemisphere.

Label the Northern Hemisphere. Label the Southern Hemisphere. Write E on the equator. Is Africa in the NORTHERN HEMISPHERE or the SOUTHERN HEMISPHERE? Color Northern Africa red. Color Southern Africa orange.

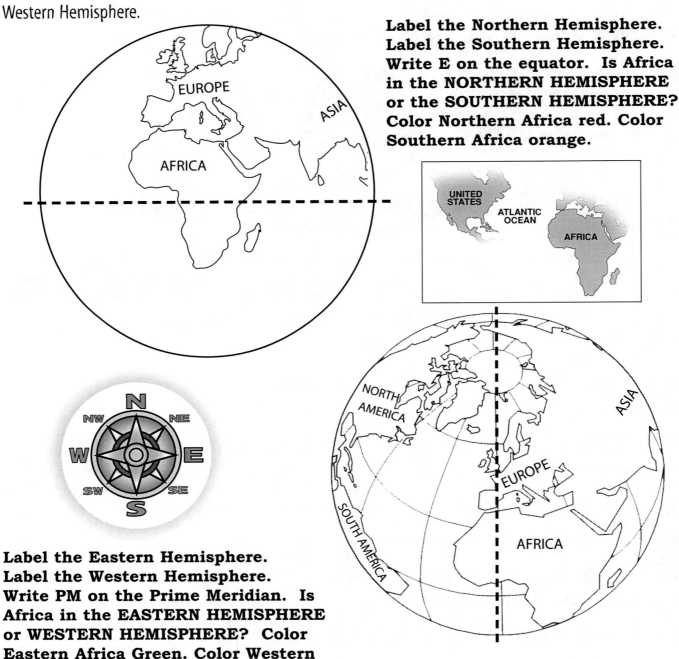

Label the Eastern Hemisphere. Label the Western Hemisphere. Write PM on the Prime Meridian. Is Africa in the EASTERN HEMISPHERE or WESTERN HEMISPHERE? Color Eastern Africa Green. Color Western Africa blue.

Answer: Africa lies in both hemispheres!

To Be or Not To Be?

African American poets introduce new thoughts and different ideas to our culture. Like the words of any other group of people, the black perspective is unique! We can learn many things by reading what others have written. As readers, we must think carefully to decide whether or not we agree with what we read. Ask a teacher or parent to help you find poetry from an African American writer. Below are just a few examples of excellent black poets.

Phillis Wheatley was a famous poet and a former slave. Her owners taught her to read and write.

Many black poets share their feelings about the difficult trials of their people, like slavery and racism, within their work. Write an original poem about a problem that you have overcome or a difficulty that you have faced. Be sure to use lots of action verbs and colorful adjectives!

Famous Black Poets:

Gwendolyn Brooks

Maya Angelou

Toni Morrison

Alice Walker

Langston Hughes

Countee Cullen

Phillis Wheatley

_____
_____
_____
_____
_____
_____
_____
_____
_____
_____
_____
_____
_____
_____
_____

Underground Railroad Word Search

Thousands of slaves escaped from their masters to find freedom in the North. Some succeeded, and some were sent back to the South. Many slaves traveled along the Underground Railroad, a network of safe places where slaves could hide and friends who could help. Harriet Tubman, known as the "Moses" of her people, was a famous "conductor" who led more than 300 slaves to freedom.

Use the Word Bank to find the words in the word search below.

Underground • fugitive • slave • abolitionist • capture • Railroad • law
Harriet Tubman • freedom • miles • North • hide • swamp • reunion
capture • African • route • South • danger • slaveowner • family
equal • fear • escape

```
L A L H S I Q C U M S S N O R T H
A B O L I T I O N I S T O Q B V P
W R A Y A D S F D B E S I U Z E K
C V S L S R E H E L V P N F T O R
E W Z A F A M S R S I O U D E H O
T N K U R O X V G J T U E R C A T
S A R Q D F S C R A I L R O A D C
E C T E J N N A O U G D S U P H U
R I E S C A P E U Y U X M T T T D
O R O S E K I M N U F U G E U W N
F F A M I L Y A D A N G E R R E O
H A R R I E T T U B M A N S E I C
V E S L A L S R E N W O E V A L S
```

Amen!

The African Baptist Church, the first known black church, was established in 1758. Today there are many kinds of black churches in America, like the African Methodist Episcopal Church and the African Orthodox Church.

Color the church and Bible.

Read All About It!

African American journalists inform the public through newspapers, television, radio, and the Internet. Journalists report the facts in a story format. They must be ready to investigate at a moment's notice! Ida B. Wells Barnett was a black investigative journalist who wrote for a black Tennessee newspaper in the 1800s. Women (especially black women) did not usually work for newspapers then, but Barnett wasn't afraid to try and step into a new world.

Barnett wrote passionately about racism and discrimination that happened in her state. Later, she traveled around America to speak to people about the need to treat black people with more respect and fairness. Barnett also became a women's suffragist and worked to give women the right to vote.

Grab your notepad and become today's fearless Ida Wells Barnett. Journalists, like Barnett, write their stories by using a basic outline. They ask who, what, where, when, and why questions. Using this format, write a story about a school event. Interview people to find out what they think about the event. Put their responses inside quotation marks.

Free States & Slave States

During the early centuries of American history, some states allowed slavery and some states did not. As of 1860, slave states included Alabama, Arkansas, Delaware, Florida, Georgia, Kentucky, Louisiana, Maryland, Mississippi, Missouri, North Carolina, South Carolina, Tennessee, Texas, and Virginia.

Free states included California, Connecticut, Illinois, Iowa, Indiana, Maine, Massachusetts, Michigan, Minnesota, New Hampshire, New Jersey, New York, Ohio, Oregon, Pennsylvania, Rhode Island, Vermont, and Wisconsin. Slaves used different routes to escape to freedom in the free Northern states, Canada, Mexico, or even the Caribbean.

Color the free states blue. Color the slave states red. Color the other states green.

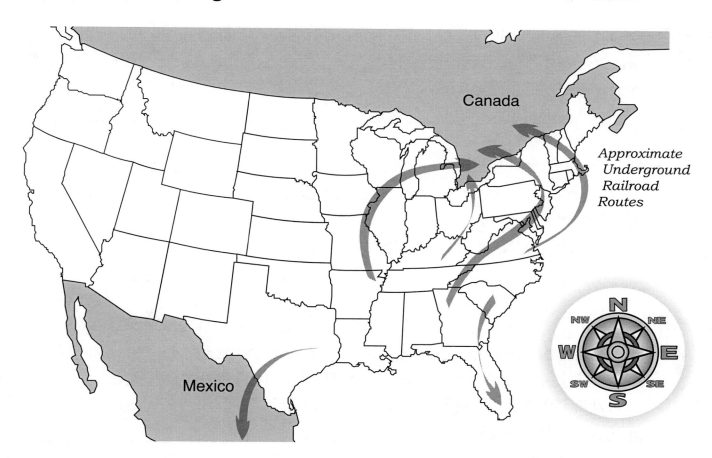

Canada

Approximate Underground Railroad Routes

Mexico

FAST FACT Harriet Tubman helped more than 300 slaves escape!

Hit That Note!

Complete the activities to learn about these famous African American performers!

1. Starting with the letter C, cross out every other letter to spell the nickname of famous blues musician W.C. Handy, who was born in 1873.

CFKARTTHYENRBOVFGTFHDEEBWLTUYEUSI

_____

2. Starting with the letter B, cross out every other letter to find out who taught the legendary Nat King Cole to play the piano at age 4.

BHTIGSHMIOOTPHSEWRV

_____

3. Starting with the letter M, cross out every other letter to discover which talented blind musician sang *Georgia on My Mind*, now the official state song of Georgia.

MRTAEYVCBHNAMROLPESSD

_____

4. Starting with the letter J, cross out every other letter to see where actor and singer Paul Robeson was educated.

JRKULTOGPEWRTSYUGNHINVMERRTSGIYTHYNAJNKDG
CTOVLFURMEBWIFAGUHNHIJVKELRTSGIYTHYULJAIWI
SOCWHSODOFLG _____

_____

_____

Answers: Father of the Blues, his mother, Ray Charles, Rutgers University and Columbia University Law School

It's Money in the Bank!

Did you know that Maggie Lena Walker became the first female bank president in 1903? She was a very famous businesswoman in her time. She headed the St. Luke Penny Savings Bank. It was founded by the Grand United Order of St. Luke, a group of people who taught African Americans how to save money and support each other in business!

Let's say that you're in college. Over the summer, you worked really hard as an intern with the National Association for the Advancement of Colored People (NAACP) bureau in Washington, D.C. You earned a lot of experience and a decent amount of money... $500 to be exact! How much will you save? How much will you spend? Solve the math problems below to find out how your earnings might be spent.

TOTAL EARNED: $500.00

I will pay back my Mom this much (A) for money I borrowed when I first started working. Thanks, Mom!   A. $20.00

    subtract A from $500 = (B)   B. _____

I will give my little brother this much money (C) for taking my phone messages while I was at work: C. $10.00

    subtract C from B = (D)   D. _____

I will spend this much (E) on a special treat for myself: E. $25.00

    subtract E from D = (F)   F. _____

I will save this much (G) for college: G. $300.00

    subtract G from F = (H)   H. _____

I will save this much (I) in a savings account to buy clothes: I. $100.00

    subtract I from H = (J)   J. _____

TOTAL STILL AVAILABLE (use answer J)   _____
TOTAL SPENT (add A, C, and E)   _____
TOTAL SAVED (add G and I)   _____

Civil Rights Movement

African Americans suffered under racial prejudice and discrimination long after they were set free by President Abraham Lincoln. Though blacks were made free citizens, they did not enjoy the same rights, privileges, or freedoms as the rest of America for decades. Blacks couldn't vote, keep weapons, run for political office, or work in certain jobs. Their schools, restaurants, neighborhoods, churches, even drinking fountains were all separate from whites.

Finally, some people decided to try to end the discrimination. Dr. Martin Luther King, Jr., a black minister, worked hard to get equal rights. He spoke for the black community, but he wanted people of all skin colors to get along with each other. Dr. King didn't want blacks or whites to isolate themselves from their country. He wanted people to work together for the common good of America. He encouraged people to help protest unfair laws through peaceful means without violence. Other civil rights heroes, like Rosa Parks and Thurgood Marshall, also helped bring about lasting change!

Follow the directions to make an Origami Peace Dove! Use the pictures to guide your steps. Keep the dove to remind yourself not to discriminate against people who are different than you. Or give the dove to someone else as a gift of peace!

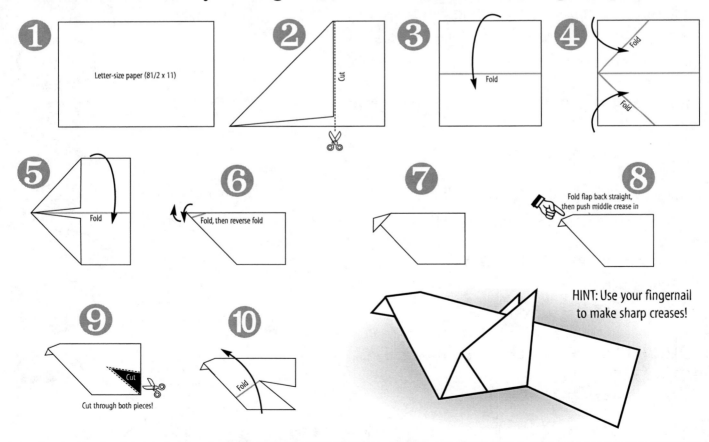

① Letter-size paper (8 1/2 x 11)

② Cut

③ Fold

④ Fold / Fold

⑤ Fold

⑥ Fold, then reverse fold

⑦

⑧ Fold flap back straight, then push middle crease in

HINT: Use your fingernail to make sharp creases!

⑨ Cut / Cut through both pieces!

⑩ Fold

"Follow The Drinking Gourd."

Slaves often communicated messages to each other through song. This famous song provides direction to slaves who wished to escape on the Underground Railroad. What do you think these clues mean?

Write your response below.

When the sun comes back and the first quail calls,
Follow the Drinking Gourd.
For the old man is waiting for to carry you to freedom,
If you follow the Drinking Gourd.
The riverbank makes a very good road,
The dead trees show you the way,
Left foot, peg foot, traveling on
Follow the Drinking Gourd.
The river ends between two hills.
Follow the Drinking Gourd.
There's another river on the other side.
Follow the Drinking Gourd.
Where the great big river meets the little river,
Follow the Drinking Gourd.
For the old man is awaiting to carry you to freedom.
If you follow the Drinking Gourd.

_____

_____

_____

_____

_____

_____

NAACP Award

The National Association for the Advancement of Colored People (NAACP) is America's oldest and largest civil rights organization. In 1915, the group began awarding Spingarn Medals to African Americans who had made great achievements.

Color the Spingarn Medal.

Spingarn Medal Recipients:

- L. Douglas Wilder
- Percy E. Sutton
- Bill Cosby
- Tom Bradley
- Lena Horne
- General Colin Powell
- Barbara Jordan
- Maya Angelou
- Dr. John Hope Franklin
- Judge A. Leon Higginbotham
- Carl Rowan
- Myrlie Evers-Williams

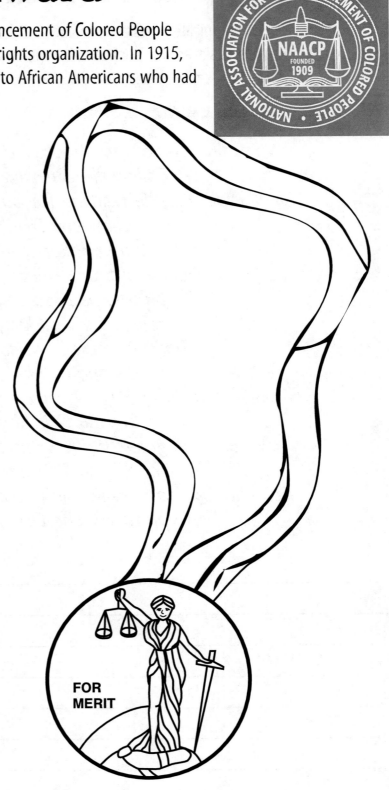

FOR MERIT

Black Firsts in the U.S. Coast Guard!

The U.S. Coast Guard was created in 1790. It used to be called the Revenue Marine. The U.S. Coast Guard is the smallest branch in the armed forces, but it is older than the U.S. Navy! African Americans have worked on ships since the early 1800s. However, they were not paid until 1831. Black seamen and seawomen have accomplished a great number of "firsts" in the U.S. Coast Guard!

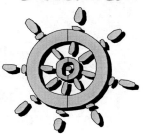

Solve the math problems below to discover the year of some historical "firsts" for blacks in the U.S. Coast Guard.

1. The Treasury Department allows free persons of color to be employed on board cutters (boats) as part of the crew.

    $6-5 =$ _____ $4+4 =$ _____ $5-2 =$ _____ $9-8 =$ _____

2. First Lieutenant Michael Healy is the first African-American to command a U.S. military vessel.

    $0+1 =$ _____ $8+0 =$ _____ $4+3 =$ _____ $7 \times 1 =$ _____

3. Richard Etheridge was the first African-American keeper of a U.S. Life-Saving Station, and he commanded the only all African-American crew in the U.S.

    $1 \times 1 =$ _____ $3+5 =$ _____ $8 \times 1 =$ _____ $8 \times 0 =$ _____

4. Erroll Brown becomes the first African-American admiral in the Coast Guard.

    $3-2 =$ _____ $3+3+3 =$ _____ $4+5 =$ _____ $4+4 =$ _____

5. The cutter (boat) Sea Cloud becomes the first U.S. military vessel to sail with a fully racially integrated crew.

    $8-7 =$ _____ $8+1 =$ _____ $8-4 =$ _____ $7-4 =$ _____

6. President Harry Truman orders the integration of the armed forces of the United States. By this time the Coast Guard had already opened up all of its rates to all qualified persons regardless of race.

    $4-3 =$ _____ $7+2 =$ _____ $2 \times 2 =$ _____ $5+3 =$ _____

Answers: 1. 1831, 2. 1877, 3. 1880, 4. 1998, 5. 1943, 6. 1948

Attention, Class!

Slaves were not allowed to read or write. It was illegal to teach black children. But many slaves learned in secret. Even a few white masters broke the law to teach their slaves so they could be of more use on the plantation.

Black educators had to teach black boys and girls how to succeed in a world that didn't want them to succeed. Education reformer Booker T. Washington was a world renowned famous black educator at the Tuskegee Institute (pronounced tusk-E-gee) in the late 1800s. He thought white people would respect black people if they became educated and were a greater benefit to American society.

Mary McLeod Bethune received an education funded by a kindly Quaker teacher. Bethune wanted other poor black children to have an opportunity to learn as she did. Starting with $1.50 in her pocket, Bethune founded Bethune-Cookman College in the early 1900s. She sold sweet potato pies and wrote letters to fund the school. Later Bethune won a Spingarn Medal for her achievements.

Make each false statement true. Cross out the false word and write the correct word in the blank.

1. Booker T. Washington worked as a gardener. _____

2. Slaves were not allowed to read or sew. _____

3. Black masters sometimes taught their slaves illegally. _____

4. Mary McLeod Bethune sold apple pies to fund her college. _____

5. Booker T. Washington taught at the Turtle Institute. _____

6. Teaching black slave children was allowed. _____

Answers: 1. False - educator, 2. False - write; 3. True; 4. False - sweet potato; 5. True; 6. True

Black History in the Zone!

Black history takes place all over America, in every state and in every time zone. The continental U.S. is divided into four time zones. There is a one-hour time difference between each zone. The earth's rotation makes the sun look like it travels from east to west, but the sun doesn't move from its fixed position!

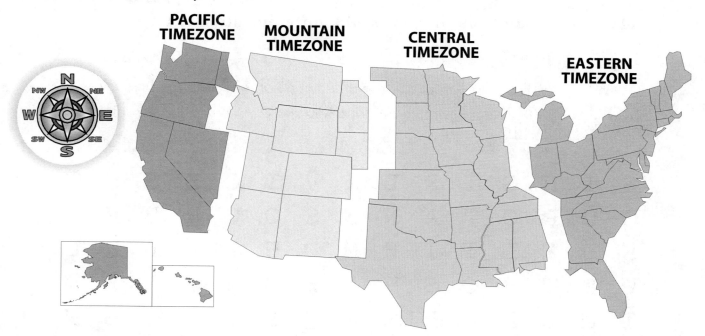

Using the time zones on the map above, answer the following questions. Then label the states found in each question.

1. In 1811, the largest slave rebellion in U.S. History took place in New Orleans, Louisiana. In what time zone did the rebellion occur? _____

2. In 1905, nine black students formed the first black fraternity, Alpha Phi Alpha, at Cornell University in New York. In what time zone did this event occur? _____

3. In 1895, Henry Flipper became the first black editor of a white newspaper, the *Nogales Sunday Herald*, in Nogales, Arizona. in which time zone did the event occur? _____

4. William Leidesdorff operated the world's first steamboat in San Francisco, California in 1847. In what time zone did this occur? _____

5. Barbara Jordan was elected to the U.S. House of Representative in 1972. This victory made her the first black Texan in the U.S. Congress. In what time zone did this event occur? _____

Answers: 1. (central; 2. Eastern 3. Mountain; 4. Pacific; 5. Central

The Great African American Word Search!

Studying black heritage can make lots of words come to mind. Some words might be new, but you have learned most these hidden words just by completing activities in this book!

Circle the words in the Word Search below. You may have to look in ALL different directions!

WORD SEARCH

Africa ● black heritage ● boycott ● civil rights
education ● emancipation ● freedom ● history
invent ● medal ● MLK ● NAACP ● pride ● racism
science ● senator ● slave ● Spingarn ● writer

```
S T H G I R L I V I C B S S T
Q U R O T A N E S O G R B F N
K U F L T I H M D U X A L R E
U D T S O S V A F R I C A E V
I M C E H M N Q P V I C B N
R A A Y Y P H C U Q Z S K A I
E L Y R O T S I H U F M H T N
T C A O B B L P X I L D E P O
I N G D B B L A D K C B R S I
R A S W E B E T F R T I I C T
W A R S O M C I B F D R T I A
R C I V L V I O K E A F A E C
S P I N G A R N S N J D G N U
Y X B W K C V F R E D O E C D
R A C M F R E E D O M M F E E
```

Black Magazine Publishing

African American publishers print books, magazines, and many other things for people to read. Black publisher John Harold Johnson borrowed $500 to start the Johnson Publishing Company in 1942. His first magazine was called *Negro Digest: A Magazine of Negro Comment*. Today, he owns the world's largest black-owned publishing company! He publishes *Ebony, Jet, Ebony Man,* and *Negro Digest*. These magazines are targeted directly for African American readers to enjoy.

Help John Harold Johnson publish his magazine. Number each box to put the steps of the publishing process in logical order.

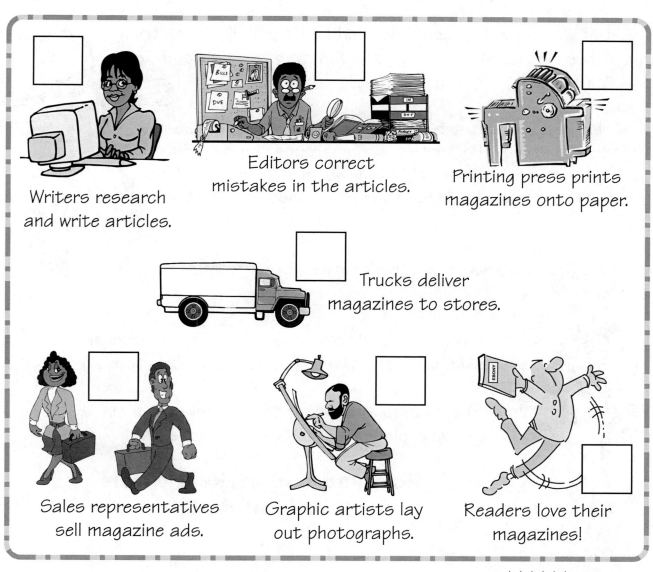

Writers research and write articles.

Editors correct mistakes in the articles.

Printing press prints magazines onto paper.

Trucks deliver magazines to stores.

Sales representatives sell magazine ads.

Graphic artists lay out photographs.

Readers love their magazines!

Answers: 1,3,5,6,4,2,7

Blacks of the Old West!

During the 1800s, many settlers traveled West in caravans of covered wagons. Black pioneers rode down those dusty paths as well, looking for a new way of life. Black pioneer children didn't have video games or soccer balls to play with so they got creative!

Follow the direction below to make a corn husk doll!

YOU WILL NEED:

• corn husks (or strips of cloth) • string • scissors

1. Select a long piece of corn husk and fold it in half. Tie a string about one inch (2.54 centimeters) down from the fold to make the doll's head.

2. Roll a husk and put it between the layers of the tied husk, next to the string. Tie another string around the longer husk, just below the rolled husk. Now your doll has arms! Tie short pieces of string at the ends of the rolled husk to make the doll's hands.

3. Make your doll's waist by tying another string around the longer husk.

4. If you want your doll to have legs, cut the longer husk up the middle. Tie the two halves at the bottom to make feet.

5. Add eyes and a nose to your doll with a marker. You could use corn silk for the doll's hair.

Now you can make a whole family of dolls!

Equality is...

Americans want equality in their country. Everyone should be treated equally without discrimination. What does equality mean to you?

Using each letter of the word "equality," write a word or phrase that describes equality.

E is for EVERYONE!

Q is for _____

U is for _____

A is for _____

L is for _____

I is for _____

T is for_____

Y is for _____

African American Trivia

Unscramble the words to discover amazing African American trivia!

WORD BANK

heart   **rookie**   **Honor**   **poet**   **People**   **Kansas**

1. Twenty-two black soldiers won the Medal of NOOHR _____ while serving in the Union Army during the Civil War!

2. The initials N.A.A.C.P. stand for National Association for the Advancement of Colored PPLEOE _____.

3. Wilt Chamberlain, NBA OORKEI _____ of the Year in 1960, was the leading team scorer for 7 years in a row.

4. Gwendolyn Brooks, noted black TEPO _____, was the first African American to win a Pulitzer Prize.

5. Stevie Wonder captured 3 out of 4 of the MYMARG _____ Awards for Male Pop Vocalist from 1973 through 1976.

6. Dr. Daniel Hale Williams performed the first open THARE _____ operation and founded Chicago's first Negro hospital, Provident.

7. The famous lawsuit Brown vs. Board of Education, which started the desegregation of American schools, took place in Topeka, SSNAKA _____.

Answers: 1. Honor; 2. People; 3. Rookie; 4. poet; 5. Grammy; 6. heart; 7. Kansas

Supreme Court Bubblegram!

The U.S. Supreme Court is the highest court in America. Only the most important cases are heard there by the Chief Justice and the eight Associate Justices. Only the president can nominate justices.

Thurgood Marshall was one of the most famous Supreme Court Justices in U.S. history. His influence on the court helped make many changes in civil rights legislation, including school desegregation.

Another famous justice is African American Clarence Thomas. He was nominated In 1990 by President George H. Bush. After the Senate approved his nomination, Clarence took his seat on October 23, 1991.

Fill in the bubblegram by using the clues below.
Some letters are already filled in for you.

1. A current black Associate Justice on the Supreme Court
2. The only person who can nominate justices for the Supreme Court
3. Thurgood Marshall helped _____ American schools
4. The number of Associate Justices on the Supreme Court
5. Black justice who was also a civil rights hero
6. The highest court in America

1. _ _ A _ _ _ _ _ H _ _ ◯
2. _ _ E _ _ _ ◯ _
3. D _ _ _ _ G _ ◯ _
4. ◯ _ _ _ T
5. _ _ _ _ G _ _ ◯ _ _ _ L
6. S _ _ _ _ _ _ _ _ U ◯

Unscramble the "bubble" letters to find out the mystery answer!

Mystery Question: Who approves the president's nominations for a justice?
Hint: You'll find them on Capitol Hill in Washington, D.C.!
Mystery Word: _____ _____ _____ _____ _____ _____

The *Amistad*

In 1839, a ship called the *Amistad* was discovered in the Long Island Sound in Connecticut. It was filled with African slaves who had taken over the ship from their masters. Connecticut authorities arrested the slaves and a few Cubans who falsely claimed to be their masters. The Spanish and Cuban governments sued the United States for a return of their "property," which included the Africans.

A lawyer named Roger Sherman Baldwin asked the Connecticut court to free the African slaves. He won the case, but it was appealed all the way to the U.S. Supreme Court. John Quincy Adams allowed the judgment to stand. The 35 black men, women, and children sailed back to their homeland!

Use information from the story to complete the crossword below.

1. The _____ took over the *Amistad* from their masters. (ACROSS)

2. The *Amistad* was found in the Long Island _____ in Connecticut. (DOWN)

3. The case was _____ in the U.S. Supreme Court. (DOWN)

4. Roger Sherman Baldwin _____ the court to free the slaves. (ACROSS)

5. The Connecticut judgment stood, and the Africans _____ home! (DOWN)

ANSWERS: 1. slaves; 2. Sound; 3. appealed; 4. asked; 5. sailed

Lincoln Memorial

In 1963, Dr. Martin Luther King Jr. delivered a famous speech in Washington, D.C. He told many people about his special dream. Dr. King dreamed of a world in which black boys and girls could play with white boys and girls peacefully. This speech was presented on the steps of the Lincoln Memorial during the March on Washington. The march was a movement where thousands of people gathered at the nation's capital to protest inequality and racism.

Color the Lincoln Memorial.

The Harlem Renaissance!

Great creativity and original thought poured out of New York City between 1919 and 1937. This era was known as the "Harlem Renaissance." During this time, many black people were confused about their place in society since becoming free. They felt left out among a mostly white European America, but they also felt a pride and love for their African roots and heritage.

These feelings surfaced in new expressions of culture. Gifted African American writers produced fiction, drama, poetry, and essays . Black musicians also heavily influenced several music forms such as jazz and blues. Black artists became more well known and studied than ever before. African American theater boomed with the popular 1921 Broadway musical *Shuffle Along*, performed by an all black cast in New York City.

Study the quote from W.E.B. Du Bois (pronounced doo-b`wah). What is the author trying to say to the reader? Write your response below.

"One ever feels his **two-ness** - an American, a Negro; two souls, two thoughts, two unreconciled stirrings: two warring ideals in one dark body, whose dogged strength alone keeps it from being torn asunder."

_____

_____

_____

_____

_____

_____

_____

Great Black Authors in History: Toni Morrison, Alice Walker, Eldridge Cleaver, Booker T. Washington, Frederick Douglass, W.E.B. Du Bois, Olaudah Equiano, James Meredit, and Toni Cade Bambara

Up, Up and Away!

During World War II, many black men left homes in farms, towns, and cities across America to volunteer as Tuskegee Airmen. They were the first black military airmen to serve in the United States armed forces. After graduating from air training, many Tuskegee Airmen became pilots, navigators, or bombardiers. Several airmen became officers, and many served in supporting ground positions.

The Tuskegee Airmen faced doubt, war, and racial discrimination. Many white Americans thought black men did not have much intelligence, courage, and patriotism. But the black airmen proved them wrong!

Follow the directions to build a paper airplane! Use the pictures to help guide your steps. Fold an 8 1/2 x 11" sheet of paper in half lengthwise. Next, fold down the corners as shown. Then fold each side down to the center again, and then again as shown in the picture. Decorate your plane to celebrate African American achievements. Be creative!

Charles "Chief" Anderson, a famous black pilot, trained Tuskegee Airmen and once took Eleanor Roosevelt up for a ride!

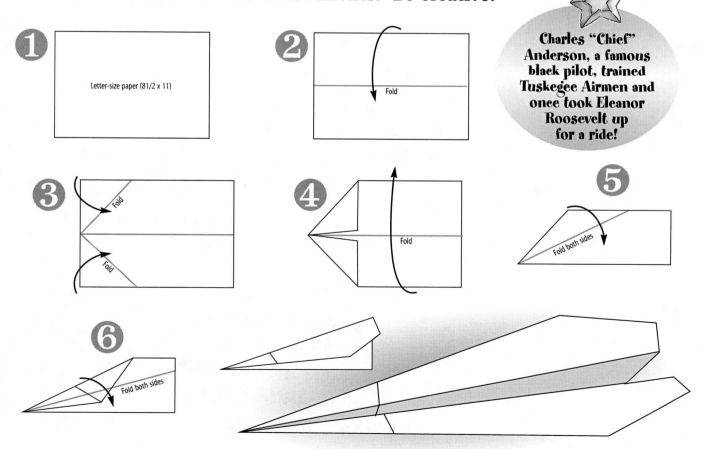

① Letter-size paper (81/2 x 11)

② Fold

③ Fold / Fold

④ Fold

⑤ Fold both sides

⑥ Fold both sides

Map to the Stars

Fugitive slaves often used star constellations in the sky to help them find the right path to freedom. Constellations are groups of stars that can represent images. A popular guidance constellation was the Drinking Gourd. Others included the Big and Little Dippers.

Complete the dot-to-dot of the constellations.

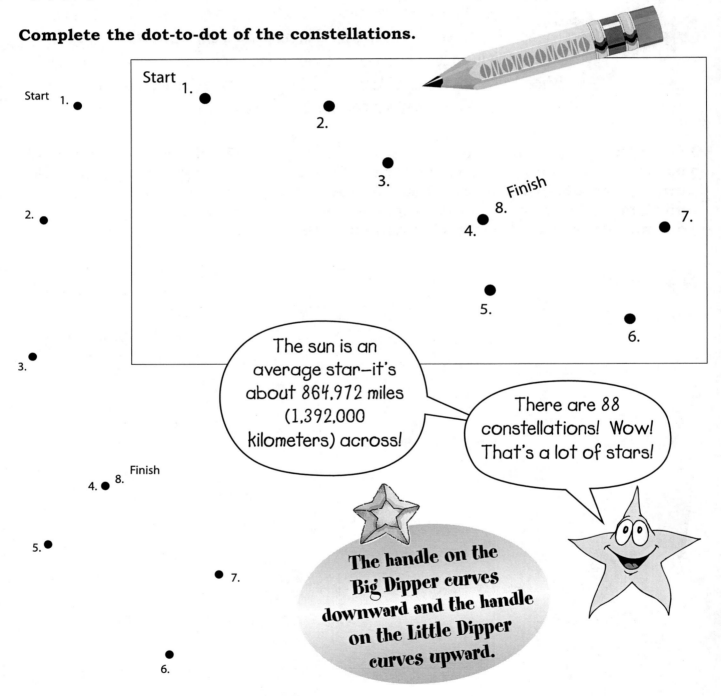

The sun is an average star–it's about 864,972 miles (1,392,000 kilometers) across!

There are 88 constellations! Wow! That's a lot of stars!

The handle on the Big Dipper curves downward and the handle on the Little Dipper curves upward.

Let's Sell Something New!

African Americans have invented many new products for many years. One innovative African American businesswoman is Sarah Breedlove McWilliams Walker. People called her Madame C.J. Walker. She was born into slavery and overcame difficult obstacles to become free. Walker invented an original treatment to straighten kinky hair. She worked very hard to make her business grow. Her hair-care products helped fill a need for millions of black people. Walker's small business turned into a million-dollar enterprise... all from one simple idea.

Think about a product that you might like to make, such as a special family cookie recipe or a new toy. It could even be a new color for a crayon! Whatever you decide, it should be something that you think is fantastic enough for people to want to buy! Answer the following questions about your "new" product in the spaces below on the assembly line.

WHAT IS YOUR
PRODUCT?
_____
_____

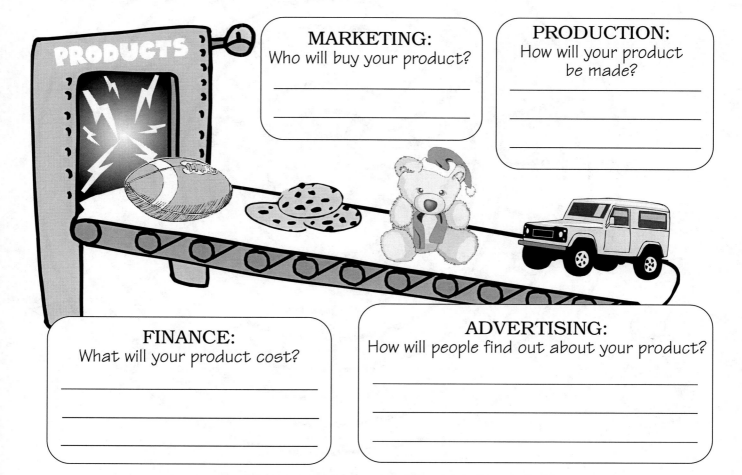

MARKETING:
Who will buy your product?
_____
_____

PRODUCTION:
How will your product
be made?
_____
_____

FINANCE:
What will your product cost?
_____
_____
_____

ADVERTISING:
How will people find out about your product?
_____
_____
_____

Black Pioneer Maze

Jean Baptiste Pointe Du Sable is one of America's greatest pioneers! He was born in Haiti in 1745 to a slave mother and pirate father. During a trip to America, a hurricane destroyed his boat and Jean Baptiste found himself on the shores of New Orleans. He traveled up the Mississippi River until he reached St. Louis. Then Jean Baptiste moved to a lonely prairie region, where the Indians refused to live. He built a small settlement and trading post for traveling explorers, hunters, trappers, settlers, and missionaries. Jean Baptiste's settlement GREW and GREW and GREW until it became the present-day city of Chicago, Illinois!

Help Jean Baptiste survive the whirling hurricane and land safely on American shores.

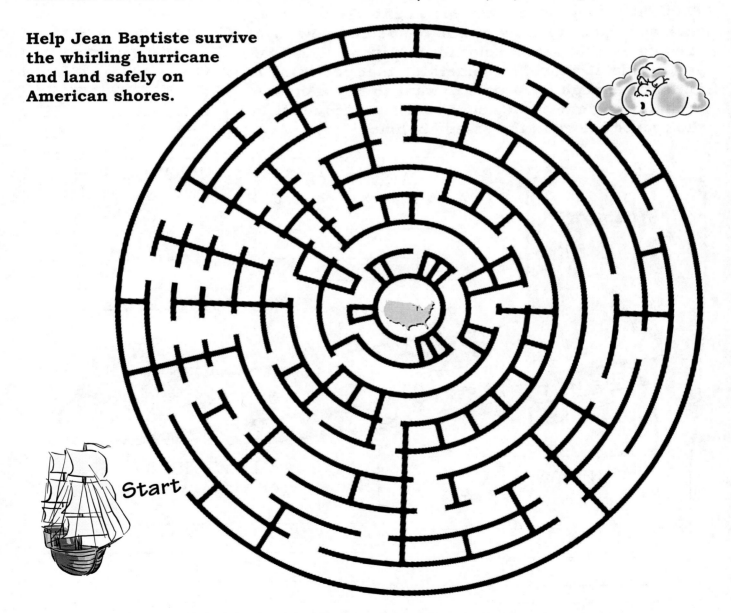

Start

Virtual N.A.A.C.P.

The National Association for the Advancement of Colored People (N.A.A.C.P.) is the oldest civil rights organization in the United States. A group of young activists formed the N.A.A.C.P. in 1909 to help improve the lives of black people. The N.A.A.C.P. leads civil right rallies and protests, maintains a Youth Council, and publishes *Crisis* magazine. The non-profit also organizes voters to register for public elections, stays involved with public policy issues to enact change in U.S. government legislation, and fights racism in the courts with legal battles.

Have you ever surfed the Internet to do research or send email? People all over the world use the Internet to find information. Many different groups and individuals maintain web sites that provide people with information about their services. Design a creative web page that tells people about the N.A.A.C.P. organization!

Countries of Africa Jumble

AFRICA

There are 52 countries on the African continent, the motherland of many African Americans.

Unscramble the names of some of these African countries. Use the Word Bank for help.

WORD BANK

Algeria	Congo	Egypt	Ethiopia
Ghana	Ivory Coast	Kenya	Liberia
Madagascar	Mali	Morocco	Nigeria
Rwanda	Senegal	Somalia	South Africa
Sudan	Tanzania	Uganda	Zimbabwe

NGCOO _____

ALERIBI _____

STHOU AARIFC _____ _____

ORIVY ASCOT _____ _____

TZIAAANN _____

ENKYA _____

MLIAASO _____

LAIM _____

MBBWZIAE _____

MCCROOO _____

NESALEG _____

ERNIGIA _____

GPTYE _____

WADRNA _____

GEALRIA _____

ANGHA _____

HIEPIATO _____

DASUN _____

DAGAMASCAR _____

DAGAUN _____

Notable People Scramble

Unscramble the last names of the faces below. Write the answers in the word wheel around the picture of each person.

1. Lorraine _____ NSHARRYBE
   Hint: This famous playwright wrote *A Raisin in the Sun* in 1959.

2. Jean Baptiste _____ _____ _____ NIPTOE UD BLESA
   Hint: This black pioneer founded a settlement which later became Chicago!

3. Leotyne _____ CEPIR
   Hint: This black opera singer once received a 42 minute ovation!

4. Mahalia _____ CKJAONS
   Hint: This gospel singer sold 1 million copies of her first album!

5. Chief Charles _____ ASONDERN
   Hint: this famous black pilot helped train America's first black fighter pilots.

NAME BANK
Anderson
Price
Jackson
Hansberry
Pointe du Sable

ANSWERS: 1: Hansberry, 2: Pointe du Sable; 3: Price, 4. Jackson, 5. Anderson

©Carole Marsh/The BIG Book of African American Activities/Page 67

Kwanzaa Spelling Bee

Good spelling is a good habit! Study the words on the page. Most all of them can be found within the activities in this book! Then fold the right half of the page under. Take a "spelling test!" Ask a friend to read the words aloud to you. Write the correct spelling on the line. When finished, unfold the page and check your spelling. How many did you spell right? Study the words you miss.

WORDS

_____ Kwanzaa

_____ ancestor

_____ creativity

_____ symbol

_____ heritage

_____ rejoice

_____ determination

_____ celebrate

_____ Africa

_____ unity

_____ present

_____ cooperation

_____ faith

_____ future

_____ principle

_____ struggle

_____ remember

_____ purpose

_____ responsibility

The Underground Railroad

Harriet Tubman helped hundreds of slaves to escape toward the North for freedom. The fugitives traveled on the "Underground Railroad." The "railroad" was a network of homes owned by people who were friendly to runaway slaves. Harriet also helped the Union Army during the Civil War. She was a spy!

The "friendly" houses below are marked with letters. Starting in the South, follow the trail to find the secret word. Color the friendly houses.

Two Make One

Match the first and last names of these famous African Americans. On a separate sheet of paper, write the reason why each person is famous.

1 Jean Baptiste _____   King Jr.

2 Countee _____   Jackson

3 Rosa _____   Morrison

4 George Washington _____   Cullen

5 Arthur _____   Parks

6 Jesse _____   Truth

7 Martin Luther _____   Ashe

8 Dr. Charles _____   Point du Sable

9 Marion _____   Owens

10 Mahalia _____   Drew

11 Toni _____   Carver

12 Sojourner _____   Jones

Answers: 1. Jean Baptiste Point du Sable; 2. Countee Cullen; 3. Rosa Parks; 4. George Washington Carver; 5. Arthur Ashe; 6. Jesse Owens; 7. Martin Luther King Jr.; 8. Dr. Charles Drew; 9. Marion Jones; 10. Mahalia Jackson; 11. Toni Morrison; 12. Sojourner Truth

Stewing in the Kitchen!

Black slave women became skilled cooks in the kitchens that belonged to their white masters. They brought many new recipes and different foods from Africa to America. Black women had to use all their resources when the pantry grew bare. They looked to nature to find some of their ingredients. Here are a few different recipes to try in your classroom or at home with a parent.

Okra is native to tropical Africa and Asia. The Egyptians cultivated okra and sent it to America with the slaves.

Fried Okra

1 lb. of fresh okra (cut in 1/4-inch rounds)
1 &1/2 cups corn meal

1/3 cup oil
Salt, pepper

Salt and pepper okra, then shake it in a brown paper sack with 1 & 1/2 cups of cornmeal until okra is all covered. Heat skillet very hot with 1/3 cup of oil. Put in okra and fry to golden brown (12 minutes or thereabout). Remove from skillet and lay okra on paper towel to absorb excess oil. Serve hot. Enough for 4 hungry folks.

Pralines

2 cups light brown sugar
2 cups granulated sugar
1/2 tsp. baking soda
2 tsp. vanilla
1 cup pecans (whole)

2 tablespoons white syrup
1 small can evaporated milk
1 cup water
2 tablespoons butter

Blend together milk, water, soda, and syrup. Blend well or milk will curdle. Stir in mixed brown and white sugar. Cook to "soft ball" stage. Remove from fire and beat until light brown. Put in vanilla, then butter and, last, pecans. Drop on wax paper and let cool. Makes about 24 medium-large patties.

Pull Apart Facts

"Pull apart" these sentences to discover cool trivia about African Americans! Write your answer on the lines provided.

1. ShirleyFranklin,mayorofAtlanta,wasthefirstAfricanAmericanfemale mayorofamajorSouthernU.S.city.

_____

_____

_____

2. Itwasagainstthelawtoteachaslavetoreadorwriteduringtheyearsof slaveryinAmerica,butmanyslaveslearnedinsecret.

_____

_____

_____

3. BayardRustinorganizedthe1963MarchonWashington,whereMartin LutherKingJr.deliveredhisfamous"IHaveADream"speechattheLincoln Memorialtoacrowdofthousands.

_____

_____

_____

4. U.S.ArmyinterpreterIsaiahDormandiedwithGeneralCusterin1876atthe BattleofLittleBigHorn.

_____

_____

_____

Amazing Firsts!

Use the Word Wheel to fill in the blanks.

WORD WHEEL

(Wheel labels: Bessie Coleman, Wole Soyinka, Black Family Summit, James Bland, Benjamin E. Mays, Wilt Chamberlain)

1. Minstrel entertainer _____ was the first black to compose a song that became an official state song. He wrote "Carry Me Back to Old Virginny."

2. In 1921, _____ became the first black woman to receive a pilot's license. She was also the first black woman stunt pilot.

3. The first _____ took place at Fisk University, Tennessee, in May 1984.

4. _____ was the first professional basketball player to score more than 3,000 points in one season and the first black to score 100 points in a single game.

5. In 1967, _____ was elected the first black president of the Atlanta Public School Board of Education.

6. In 1986, Nigerian playwright, poet, and novelist _____ became the first African to win a Nobel Prize for literature.

Answers: James Bland, Bessie Coleman, Black Family Summit, Wilt Chamberlain, Benjamin E. Mays, Wole Soyinka

African Americans Word Wizards

Use the Word Bank to help fill in the missing letters and learn the names of some skilled Word Wizards!

WORD BANK

Alice Walker, fiction writer ● William Wells Brown, novelist
Paul Laurence Dunbar, poet ● William Cooper Nell, historical writer
Benjamin Griffith Brawley, non-fiction author

AUL LA R NC

DUNB R

Somalia is the only country on Earth where all the citizens speak one language, Somali.

More than 1,000 different languages are spoken in Africa.

BE JA IN

G I FITH RAWL Y

I LIAM

C OP R NEL L

A ICE AL ER

The Berbers of North Africa have no written form of their language.

WILLI M

W LLS BR WN

Wildlife Matching

Match the animals, which are all native to Africa, with their correct pictures. Color the animals.

Cheetah

Buffalo

Lion

Gazelle

Penguin

Swan

Frog

Crocodile

Elephant

Giraffe

Hyena

Cheetahs are the fastest land animals on earth. They can run between 60 and 70 miles per hour!

Blacks in the Workplace

One great advantage to being an American is that we can all decide what we want to do with our lives. No one tells us where we have to stay in life. Many famous African American achievers decided what career they wanted to have and then overcame obstacles with hard work to make it happen. Most importantly, these people decided that no one could distract them from their goals. You can do this too!

Read each question. Use the Word Bank to fill in the blanks below.

WORD BANK

money	orators	Cross	woman
nurse	slavery	land	positions

1. Shirley Franklin served in many different city government _____ before Atlanta citizens elected her mayor in 2002. She waited a long time to become mayor, but chose to stay busy learning her whole life. Now Franklin is the first African American _____ to serve as mayor of a major U.S. city!

2. Frederick Douglass did not have the opportunity to attend school, like many children do today, because he was black. After escaping from _____, he educated himself and became one of the greatest _____ in U.S. history.

3. Amos Fortune served as a slave for a long time. He worked hard, saved his _____ and was finally able to buy his freedom. Fortune eventually bought the freedom of his wife and saved enough to buy his own plot of _____.

4. Susie King Taylor decided that she wanted to become a _____ like Clara Barton, founder of the American Red _____. She wanted to help the black soldiers who were wounded in the Civil War. Taylor served until the war ended.

Choose two careers. Write one thing you can do to help prepare for each career.

_____	_____
Career Choice	How to Prepare

_____	_____
Career Choice	How to Prepare

Answers: 1. positions, woman; 2. slavery, orators; 3. money, land; 4. nurse, Cross

Juneteenth Crossword

On June 19, 1865, **WSNE** _____ of the Emancipation Proclamation signed by President Abraham Lincoln finally arrived in Texas, after two-and-a-half years! Major General Gordon Granger read an official announcement in Galveston, Texas, and then **LAVSES** _____ were **EEFR** _____ to leave their masters! The slaves celebrated this new freedom by praying, feasting, dancing, and singing!

Today Juneteenth is an unofficial **LIHAYOD** _____ observed by many African Americans. When **ASTEX** _____ slaves migrated, they spread the **JETUENTNEH** _____ tradition across the United States. It is now a holiday in Texas, Iowa, Idaho, California, Wyoming, and several other states.

WORD BANK
free Texas Juneteenth
slaves news holiday

Unscramble the words in the paragraphs above. Then use the Word Bank to solve the crossword puzzle.

J U N E T E E N T H

African Americans celebrate Juneteenth in much the same style as the Fourth of July.

Answers: news, slaves, free, holiday, Texas, Juneteenth

Mirror, Mirror On the Wall

Swahili is an African language. Find the meaning of each Swahili word by holding this page up to a mirror. Write the meanings on the lines provided.

IMANI (*ee-MAH-nee*)

believing in yourself

_____

KUUMBA (*koo-OO-mbah*)

a new way to do something

_____

PRONUNCIATIONS

a = *ah* as in *father*
e = *a* as in *day*
i = *ee* as in *free*
o = *o* as in *go*
u = *oo* as in *too*

NIA (*NEE-ah*)

purposeful living

_____

UJIMA (*oo-JEE-mah*)

working together

_____

The language of Swahili is formally called Kiswahili!

Harambee! (hah-rahm-BEH!) Let's pull together!

UMOJA (*oo-MOH-jah*)

unity

_____

Buzzing Around Black Athletes!

African Americans also show their talent in the professional sports arena. Black athletes participate in basketball, soccer, football, baseball, golf, tennis, and other sports!

Find the answers to the questions by buzzing through the maze!

1. Black basketball star _____ _____ helped the Chicago Bulls win 5 NBA championships!

2. The first African American to play baseball in the major leagues was _____ _____! He played for the Brooklyn Dodgers.

3. African American sisters _____ and _____ _____ play professional tennis!

4. Golfer _____ _____ is a roaring good black athlete!

5. Riding jockey _____ _____ rode a horse named Aristides in the Kentucky Derby!

6. Chicago Bears running back _____ _____ is remembered as one of the greatest football players of all time!

7. African American boxer _____ _____ floated like a butterfly and stung like a bee.

8. WNBA black basketball star _____ _____ was named both WNBA Most Valuable Player and Defensive Player of the Year in 2000.

Jackie Robinson

Tiger Woods

Start here

Venus & Serena Williams

Michael Jordan

Oliver Lewis

Sheryl Swoopes

Walter Payton

Muhammed Ali

Answers: 1. Michael Jordan, 2. Jackie Robinson, 3. Venus and Serena Williams, 4. Tiger Woods, 5. Oliver Lewis, 6. Walter Payton, 7. Muhammed Ali, 8. Sheryl Swoopes

Collegiate Word Search

Many historically black colleges and universities educate students in the United States. Here are some examples of good schools that teach students how to succeed in today's world.

Find the words.

```
M O R E H O U S E C O L L E G E A N T C Y
O Y G A Y T I S R E V I N U W A H S U G Z
R T O N S B E P A G Z S N H A P A E S X N
R I H S P N S Y R X A P E X L S D G K L O
I S A F I S K U N I V E R S I T Y E E H E
S R N X O O P Y G G B L D U N M E L G L G
B E T H U N E C O O K M A N C O L L E G E
R V L P H N Q R S C O A D I O J G O E J L
O I B M S L L E P U L N S V L J F C U K L
W N G P A T T L E N K C G L N T O T N I O
N U E D P U I L L I O O R L U I S T I G C
C D P X A S N U F H C L C O N T M E V F N
O R Y N R M D I L O G L D C I L B N E X A
L A E P O G E E V X B E L C V T M N R U M
L W R Y A Y E O L E D G L O E I T E S V L
E O N I N P C O L O R E W E R I O B I G L
G H D S L E G E L C B S W G S I K C T C I
E B E G A C N I O D C S I T I S E O Y L T
U D S W G O W M P E N E M T T P C Y N L S
T W K R O B X Z L V C M O E Y P N D M U Q
```

Send Me!

The United States Postal Service issues new stamps each year. Some stamps honor great Americans.

Choose a great African American! Design a stamp to honor his or her achievements. Write some of this person's contributions to America.

Name _____

Contributions _____

_____

Flag Find!

How many bendera flags can you find in this picture? Write your answer in the box. Color the picture.

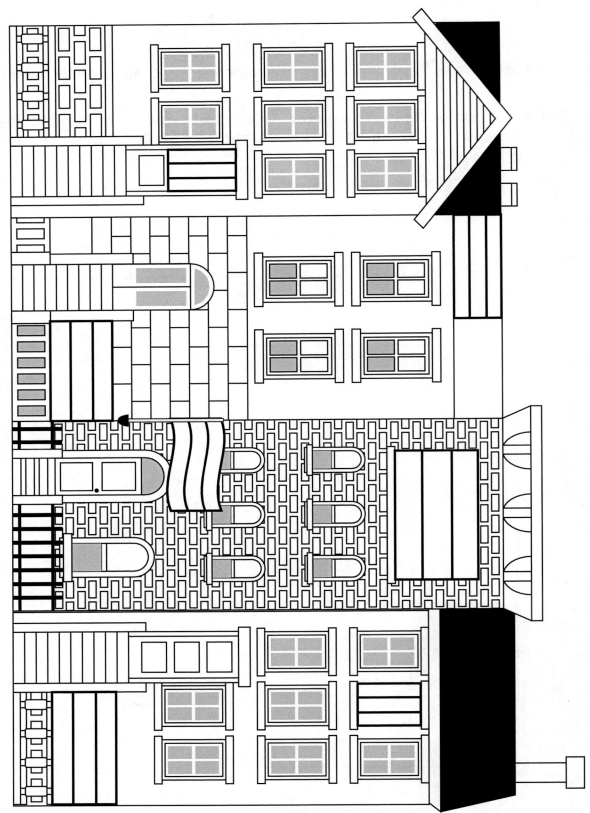

Answer: 7

Color Me!

African Geo-Facts

Read these fascinating tidbits of information about African geography.
Underline each noun and circle each verb.

The Continent of Africa

- Africa is the second largest continent on Earth. It covers about 11,699,000 square miles (30,330,000 square km)!

- The Republic of Sudan, located in northeastern Africa, is the largest country of the African continent. The Seychelles is the smallest African country.

- Mount Kilimanjaro in Tanzania is the highest point in Africa. Lake 'Asal in Djibouti is the lowest point.

- The northernmost tip is Cape Blanc in Tunisia, and the southernmost tip is Cape Agulhas in South Africa.

- Lake Victoria is the largest lake in Africa and the world's second largest freshwater lake. Lake Tanganyika is the deepest lake in Africa; its greatest depth is 4,710 feet (1,436 m).

- The Nile, which drains northeastern Africa, is the longest river in Africa and in the world at 4,132 miles (6,650 km).

- Namib Desert is the world's oldest desert.

- The Fish River Canyon in Namibia is the second largest canyon in the world.

- The Sahara Desert is expanding southwards at an average of a half-mile (0.8 km) each month.

Birmingham Civil Rights Institute

The Birmingham Civil Rights Institute is a museum and educational center in Birmingham, Alabama that exhibits the fight for civil rights in the United States and beyond. The journey includes the era of segregation, the Civil Rights Movement of the 1950s and 1960s, and the worldwide struggle for civil and human rights. The Institute's projects and services involve research and encourage discussion on human rights in America and around the world.

Use the Word Wheel to fill in the blanks.

WORD WHEEL

Alabama · research · discussion · world · segregation · Movement

1. The Birmingham Civil Rights Institute promotes _____ about civil and human rights.

2. The museum features exhibits about civil rights in the United States and around the _____.

3. The Birmingham Civil Rights Institute is located in Birmingham, _____.

4. Scholars at the Institute continue to learn about civil rights through _____.

5. One major exhibit at the museum describes the era of _____.

6. The Civil Rights _____ took place during the 1950s and 1960s.

Answers: 1-discussion; 2- world; 3-Alabama; 4-research; 5-segregation; 6-Movement

Own the Microphone!

African American musicians have created new twists with soulful, energetic songs throughout the decades. Black voices can be heard loud and proud in every type of music; they have influenced jazz, rhythm and blues, rap, swing, soul, and funk!

Use the Word Bank to match each singer with the correct song.

___ 1. Billie Holiday   HINT: Rain, snow, sleet...

___ 2. Run-D.M.C.   HINT: Which direction?

___ 3. Ella Fitzgerald   HINT: You crack me up!

___ 4. Stevie Wonder   HINT: Not twice!

___ 5. Nat "King" Cole   HINT: I never forget a face.

___ 6. Aretha Franklin   HINT: All I want is a little...

___ 7. Duke Ellington   HINT: Twirl around!

___ 8. Michael Jackson   HINT: Rhymes with chiller!

___ 9. Marvin Gaye   HINT: What's happening?

___ 10. Louis Armstrong   HINT: Earth rocks!

ANSWER BANK

(A) For Once In My Life

(B) What's Going On

(C) Respect

(D) Stormy Weather

(E) Thriller

(F) Unforgettable

(G) My Funny Valentine

(H) Walk This Way

(I) What A Wonderful World

(J) It Don't Mean A Thing, If It Ain't Got that Swing

Answers: 1. D; 2. H; 3. G; 4. A; 5. F; 6. C; 7. J; 8. E; 9. B; 10. I

State Shapes!

Look at the pictures to answer each question. Write your answer on the line. Color each picture.

1. Which state legalized slavery in 1661?

Virginia
Kentucky
Tennessee

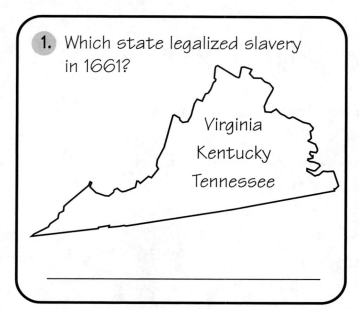

_____

2. In which state, is the African American community of Harlem located?

New York
New Jersey
Rhode Island

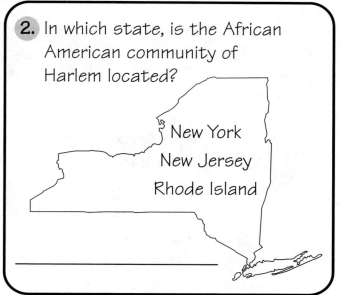

_____

3. In which country was the NAACP (National Association for the Advancement of Colored People) founded?

Canada
United States
Mexico

_____

4. Where did the March on Washington take place in 1963?

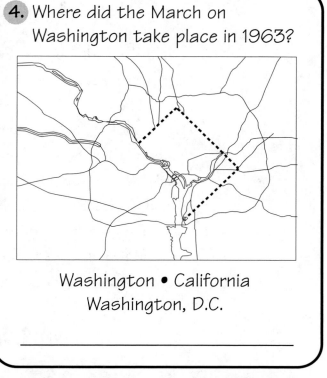

Washington • California
Washington, D.C.

_____

Answers: 1-Virginia; 2-New York; 3-Canada; 4-Washington, D.C.

The History of Kwanzaa

**Read the story. Highlight all the nouns yellow.
Underline all the verbs in red.**

Once there was a man named Maulana Karenga. He was a very intelligent African American scholar. Maulana looked around his world and saw racial inequality, the battle for civil rights, and prejudice. He believed that African Americans needed to learn more about their African history. He knew that Africans would unite into a stronger community if they understood and honored their common ancestry.

In 1966, Maulana Karenga decided to combine many different African customs and traditions into one special holiday called Kwanzaa. The word Kwanzaa means "first fruits" in Swahili, an African language. Many families all around the world observe Kwanzaa, an African American holiday celebrated for seven days, from December 26 to January I.

The celebration of Kwanzaa focuses on Seven Principles (*Nguzo Saba*). These principles are taught by using the Seven Symbols. Families spread the *mkeka* on a low table. The *kinara* and *kikombe cha umoja* are placed in the center. The *muhindi* are placed around the *kinara*. The *mishumaa saba* are set to the far right. The *zawadi* and *mazao* go on the *mkeka*. The symbols and principles are designed to pull the African American community together and to grow stronger as one body.

Code Red! Revolt!

Solve the codes to find out the names of these famous slaves who led rebellions in the early 1800s.

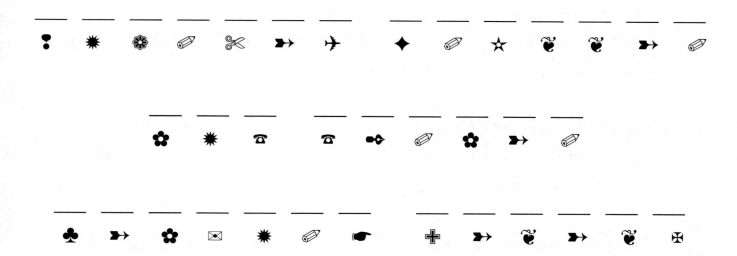

The largest slave rebellion in U.S. history took place in Louisiana in 1811. More than 300 slaves revolted by killing white people and burning down plantations. Soldiers stopped them in New Orleans and executed rebels by the dozens.

Answers: Gabriel Prosser, Nat Turner, Denmark Vesey

Order In The Court!

African American history is full of important court cases and new laws. These cases and new laws helped change the treatment of African Americans.

Order! Order! Order in the court! These dates are all mixed up! Number the events on the timeline in chronological order.

In 1967, Thurgood Marshall was the first African American appointed to the U.S. Supreme Court.

_____ U.S. Supreme Court declares segregated public schools unconstitutional in the *Brown vs. Board of Education* court case. (1954)

_____ Virginian slave Dred Scott sues for his freedom (and his family's freedom) on the grounds that his master had moved to a free state. The U.S. Supreme Court rules against him and further states that black people are an "inferior class" that has no rights that white people should respect. (1846)

_____ Equal Employment Opportunity Act passes, reducing job discrimination against people of all races, religions, and genders in the United States. (1972)

_____ Congress passes the Voting Rights Act, which allows blacks to vote freely and unhindered. (1965)

_____ U.S. Supreme Court legalizes separate but equal facilities for blacks and whites in the *Plessy vs. Ferguson* court case. (1896)

Answers: 3, 1, 5, 4, 2

Notable Black Doctors!

- One of the first blacks in America known to work with medicine was the black slave Oneisimus who developed an antidote for smallpox

- Dr. Theodore Lawless helped thousands who suffered from various skin ailments. He also taught medicine at Northwestern University, his alma mater, for more than fifteen years

- Doctor Rebecca Lee was one of the first black doctors in the United States

- Dr. James Durham was the first black doctor in America.

- Dr. Ulysses Grant Dailey was known for skill in the operating room.

- Dr. Daniel Hale Williams performed the world's first successful open-heart operation in 1893. Dr. Williams also founded the black Provident Hospital in Chicago, Illinois and the first black nursing school in Washington, D.C.

Match the black doctors below with their most notable medical accomplishment!

1. Dr. Theodore Lawless
2. Dr. Ulysses Grant Dailey
3. Dr. Daniel Hale Williams
4. Dr. Rebecca Lee
5. Oneisimus
6. Dr. James Durham

A. one of world's leading dermatologists
B. first black female to earn a medical degree
C. performed first successful open heart surgery in the world
D. slave who developed smallpox antidote
E. first American black doctor
F. skilled black surgeon

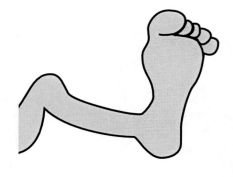

Answers: 1.A; 2.F; 3.C; 4.B; 5.D; 6.E

Scrapbook of...

Check out these pictures of African American events in history. Are you familiar with all of them? Research some more events and draw them in the spaces provided. Create your own scrapbook of African American history!

Use the blank boxes to get started.

(Sorting tobacco) T.B. Williams Co., Richmond, VA (1899)

16th Street Baptist Church, Birmingham, AL

African American Soldiers
Monument, Chicago, IL

African American History

Howard University
Washington, D.C. (1979)

Colored pool hall, Beale St., Memphis TN (1939)

Frederick Douglass House, Wash., D.C. (1963)

Abolitionist Crossword

Use the Word Bank to solve the crossword puzzle.

WORD BANK

North   free   orator   Lincoln   illegal

ACROSS

1. Many black and white abolitionists worked to make slavery _____.
2. Frederick Douglass was a famous _____ who delivered speeches against slavery.

DOWN

3. Black abolitionists Frederick Douglass and Sojourner Truth both advised President Abraham _____ on how to improve treatment of black people.
4. The Emancipation Proclamation of 1863 finally set the slaves _____.
5. Two newspapers, Freedom's Journal and the _____ Star, published articles about the evils of slavery.

Answers: 1-illegal; 2-orator; 3-Lincoln; 4-free; 5-North

Amazing African Americans!

Acrostic poems are composed by writing a word or phrase that starts with each letter of a word. See if you can write your own acrostic poem about African Americans.

Next to every letter, write a word or phrase that describes African American people. The first letter is done for you. Now let's see what you can do!

A is for Around the Nation!

F is for _____

R is for _____

I is for _____

C is for _____

A is for _____

N is for _____

A is for _____

M is for _____

E is for _____

R is for _____

I is for _____

C is for _____

A is for _____

N is for _____

Official
BLACK HERITAGE
BIG ACTIVITY BOOK
Certificate

Presented to:

_____

This certificate verifies that the above named is officially an intellectual of The African American Experience!

_____
Signature

_____
Date